Hea

full

it c

MW01643679

pleasing God requires adding to our faith, when fulfilment and purpose are already ours in Jesus. Spiritual growth happens when we say 'No' to earthly desire and practice, and set our focus on Christ alone. After all, we are only temporary residents here. The book is full of advice on how to 'set our minds on things above', which ensures that we will never lose sight of Jesus. Excellent for personal meditation, *Heavenly Minded* is also perfect for studying with others.

– CATHERINE CAMPBELL, author of *God Isn't Finished With You Yet*, and *Broken Works Best*

In this small book, you get a devotion, commentary, and Bible study all-in-one! This was just the reminder I needed to re-orient my heart heavenward, and I trust it will be just what you need as well. If you feel the pull of the world on your heart and mind, do yourself a favor and prayerfully read this book with heart and Bible open.

– KRISTIE ANYABWILE, Bible teacher, author

In the midst of our daily lives and earthly cares, what does it mean to set our minds on things above? In her new book, *Heavenly Minded*, Mary Willson Hannah unpacks wisdom from the book of Colossians as a guide to show us the importance and challenge of embracing our new identity in Christ. With biblical depth and insight, she warmly invites us to lift our gaze from our earthly circumstances and fix our eyes on heavenly realities.

– MELISSA KRUGER, author and vice president of discipleship programming at The Gospel Coalition

In this quick and compelling read, Mary Willson Hannah—true to form—offers thoughts that are smart, convicting, and theologically rich. A good fit for individual devotions, a small group Bible study, or Sunday school, this is a wonderful reminder of what Christians are looking forward to—and how that changes the way we live today.

– SARAH EEKHOFF ZYLSTRA, senior writer and faith-and-work editor at The Gospel Coalition

Heavenly Minded

Heavenly Minded

MARY WILLSON HANNAH

Unless otherwise stated, Scripture quotations are from The Holy Bible, English Standard Version, ESV®. Text Edition: [illegible] Copyright © 2001 by Crossway Bibles, a publishing ministry of Good News Publishers. Used by permission. All rights reserved.

Copyright © 2023 by Mary Willson Hannah

First published in Great Britain in 2023

The right of Mary Willson Hannah to be identified as the Author of this Work has been asserted by her in accordance with the Copyright, Designs and Patents Act 1988.

All rights reserved. No part of this publication may be reproduced, stored in a retrieval system or transmitted in any form or by any means, electronic, mechanical, photocopying, recording or otherwise, without the prior permission of the publisher or the Copyright Licensing Agency.

British Library Cataloguing in Publication Data
A record for this book is available from the British Library

ISBN: 9781913896522

Designed by Jude May

Cover image © zmshv | iStock
Printed in Denmark

10Publishing, a division of 10ofthose.com
Unit C, Tomlinson Road, Leyland, PR25 2DY, England
Email: info@10ofthose.com
Website: www.10ofthose.com

1 3 5 7 10 8 6 4 2

If then you have been raised with Christ, seek the things that are above, where Christ is, seated at the right hand of God. Set your minds on things that are above, not on things that are on earth. For you have died, and your life is hidden with Christ in God. When Christ who is your life appears, then you also will appear with him in glory (Col. 3:1–4).

Contents

PART 1:

The Need to Be Heavenly Minded

1

The Call

It seems odd to suggest that in order for people to live meaningful and productive lives on earth, they must focus on other-worldly things. But that's precisely what the Bible teaches.

The Bible is written largely for believers—believers like you and me who struggle with many trials and tribulations here on earth. It's only natural for human beings, living in this world, to be thinking about things in this world. It's normal that we give thought to our physical and emotional health, our appearance, our possessions, our relationships, our occupations, our failures, our successes. To manage them well, we have to think about them! But the Bible consistently tells believers that worldly things can't be our priority. We must concern ourselves less with money, careers, politics, and sport—they can't be our main focus in life. We must concern ourselves more with our Savior, our identity and our final destination. Only then will we gain true joy, peace and hope. Heavenly mindedness, rather than worldly mindedness, is key to the Christian life.

There are many places where Scripture stresses the necessity of heavenly mindedness. One of the more famous passages is found in Paul's letter to the church in Colossae. In Colossians 3:1–4, he writes:

> *If then you have been raised with Christ, seek the things that are above, where Christ is, seated at the right hand of God. Set your minds on things that are above, not on things that are on earth. For you have died, and your life is hidden with Christ in God. When Christ who is your life appears, then you also will appear with him in glory (Col. 3:1–4).*

Paul urges us to cultivate this heavenly mindedness in our lives. It is vital. It combats joy-sapping fear.

It heals Christ-dishonoring divisions. It undercuts soul-crushing doubts. And who doesn't want that?

"Jesus plus"

Have you ever been part of a local church in crisis? Serious troubles plagued the young Colossian church. Paul had never met these Christians face to face, but he was deeply concerned for them. Some in this local congregation had come to believe the secret to spiritual growth was to be found, not in Christ, but in mystical religious practices and rigorous self-discipline. Paul was distressed! So distressed, in fact, that he wrote them a letter from prison.

Paul most likely caught wind of these troubles from his ministry partner, Epaphras (see Phlm. 23). It was Epaphras who first proclaimed the gospel in his home town of Colossae (Col. 1:7–8; 4:12). And it was Epaphras who seems to have heard that a group of false teachers had infiltrated that congregation and caused divisions among them (Col. 2:16–19).

These false teachers claimed that for believers to mature and experience spiritual satisfaction, they needed to add to the simple gospel of the Lord Jesus Christ. They promoted a sort of

"Jesus plus" religion, arguing that, *in addition to trusting in Jesus Christ*, Christians should strive for super-spiritual "wisdom" and commit to certain religious regimens, such as treating their bodies harshly (Col. 2:16–23). You can visualize their understanding of true spiritual life as a pie chart: rather than comprising the whole pie, Jesus and his gospel contributed only one part, even if a large part.

In essence, these false teachers were claiming that their "Jesus plus" program was the key to true spiritual maturity. They intended to promote it and so take the Colossian congregation captive by worldly priorities and methods (Col. 2:8, 23), rather than heavenly ones.

Sound familiar? It's a chronic temptation of the church in every generation to distort the gospel with some form of "Jesus plus" religion. A simple perusal of hot-topic debates among believers on social media illustrates these tendencies. We emphasize choice issues in a manner that sets them up as a litmus test for "authentic" or "mature" faith, and then we cancel anyone who fails our test. "I can't imagine that a *real* Christian could ever vote for *that* political party," we sometimes say. "How could a genuine believer not make *such-and-such* social issue their main priority?" Or, "How could a proper Christian go to *that* church or hold *that* opinion?"

Even when we might score 100% on a doctrine quiz, our "Jesus plus" attitudes and actions betray what we actually believe: that Christianity is *really* about following a set of moral rules, belonging to a particular church tribe, achieving certain life goals, or advocating for the right social cause (or avoiding *any* apparent support for *any* social cause). With this sort of in-or-out, hierarchal attitude, we inevitably create a religious "caste" system. We each can end up passing judgment on other believers who don't adhere to our chosen priorities in the precise way we demand. None of us is immune to being deceived by a "Jesus plus" mindset.

The call to cultivate heavenly mindedness comes to us smack-dab in the middle of such temptations. So, if we're to answer that call, we've got no alternative but to face up to the challenge it brings.

2

The Challenge

No one wants a doctor who skirts around a tough diagnosis; we want them to tell us the truth, the whole truth, and nothing but the truth. The Apostle Paul confronts the problem head-on, unmasking the enslaving emptiness of "Jesus plus" religion. He calls believers—you and me—to trust Jesus Christ's sufficiency for our full salvation, from new birth all the way to glory (Col. 2:6–7). He urges us to embrace and enjoy Christ as our ongoing source of life and fullness.

In Colossians 3:1–4 we discover the heart of Paul's call to Christ-centered living. Here we find no "adding to," no pushing aside of Jesus Christ. Jesus is center stage. Paul is convinced that Christ is the sum of the Christian life. He fills the whole pie chart. Christ is the starting point, the ending point, and every point in between. It's all about Jesus.

That's why growing as a Christian means becoming more like Jesus Christ, "from one degree of glory to another" (2 Cor. 3:18). Do we become more like Jesus in our own strength or on our own merits? Absolutely not! We become more like Jesus by taking hold of the privileges he has secured for us, privileges that are already ours in him. Believers have been united with Christ. We are already one with him. So it stands to reason that, in response, we would desire to live in line with this new identity. It stands to reason that we would focus our hearts and minds on Jesus, who is now in heaven. To put it simply: the antidote to "Jesus plus" religion and the key to Christian growth is heavenly mindedness.

Embracing Heavenly Mindedness

Think for a moment about some goal you worked long and hard to achieve. Maybe for you it was learning a language, or competing in a contest, or finishing a project, or remaining faithful in a difficult relationship. Reaching that goal required *setting your mind on it*, right? You had to keep your eyes on the prize. And that involved self-control and proactive training.

Paul doesn't actually use the word "heaven" in Colossians 3:1–4, but he clearly has heaven in mind as he talks about the "things that are above" (3:1, 2). By repeating the command to seek what is above and to set our minds on what is above, Paul stresses the importance of heavenly mindedness and implicitly acknowledges its challenge. What does it mean to look heavenward? Well, it means to turn to Christ, who is seated in heaven. Turn to the eternal things of God. Turn to the enduring city whose builder and maker is God. Turn to what is good and holy. Turn to the everlasting throne of God.

Paul takes for granted that believers must *choose* what to seek and what to contemplate. If you're a believer in Jesus Christ, your mind should belong to the Lord. But rather than imagining that our mind will turn to the Lord on autopilot, we must train our mind to do so. This doesn't mean that we grit our teeth to make ourselves think about Jesus with a cold or begrudging heart. Of course not! Setting our mind on heaven entails giving our heart over to the Lord, since what we love (and hate) shapes how we think. Elsewhere Paul explains that whereas "the mind that is set on the flesh is hostile to God" and leads to death (Rom. 8:7, 6), those who are "in Christ Jesus" (Rom. 8:1) are set free to "set their minds on the things of the Spirit" (Rom. 8:5). So, by the Spirit's power, believers in Christ Jesus are liberated to choose our mindset (see 1 Pet. 1:13). That is, we're not only redeemed *from* enslavement to worldly thinking, but *for* setting our mind actively on what is above.

Jesus himself supremely exemplifies the sort of heavenly mindedness that equips human beings for maximum satisfaction and usefulness in this world. And he embraced this heavenly mindedness amid fierce struggle. He humbly receives his heavenly Father's loving pleasure in him (Matt. 3:17). He consistently relies on his heavenly Father's blessing throughout his ministry (Matt. 14:19). The nearness of the kingdom of heaven shapes his preaching (Matt. 4:17), and the superiority of heaven's treasures suffuses his teaching (Matt. 6:20). Jesus even endures the injustice of Calvary by entrusting himself to his heavenly Judge (1 Pet. 2:23). Because we believers are united with Christ, the same heavenly mindedness also equips us to persevere amid life's hardships. Following the pattern our Savior set, we are instructed and empowered even to bless the very ones who curse us (1 Pet. 3:9; Acts 7:59–60).

Rejecting Worldly Mindedness

Embracing one thing usually means rejecting something else. Saying "yes" to a new fitness regime means saying "no" to indulging in your favorite unhealthy foods. (Well, it usually does!) Saying "yes" to one professional opportunity means saying "no" to others. Embracing marriage to one spouse means rejecting all other would-be suiters. In Colossians 3:1–2, we see that heavenly mindedness is no different. Seeking "the things that are above," has to replace setting our hearts and minds "on things that are on earth" (Col 3:2; Phil. 3:19).

You cannot be both a heavenly minded person and a worldly person. If you are heavenly minded, you will renounce worldliness in your thinking, including "Jesus plus" religion. Jesus regularly taught his hearers and followers to renounce worldliness: "You cannot serve God and money" (Matt. 6:24). As masters, the two are mutually exclusive. "Do not have Jesus Christ on your lips, and the world in your heart," quipped Ignatius of Antioch (see 1 John 2:15–17).[1]

The situation at Colossae illustrates that a worldly mindset can get a foothold in an entire congregation. Charles Spurgeon's assessment of the church in his day still rings true: "One reason why the church of God at this present moment has so little influence over the world is because the world has so much influence over the church."[2] Ouch.

Sadly, in our own time we see in vivid colors a tell-tale symptom of the church being driven by worldliness: *a spirit of divisiveness*. Think for a moment about the division you can observe among professing Christians. Consider the examples you see of Christians showing favoritism toward people of their own ethnic and cultural background, while minimizing the concerns of their brothers and sisters from other backgrounds. Consider what you notice on social media, where people who take the name of Christ in their "about me" section belittle those who think differently

---

1. Ignatius of Antioch, *Epistle to the Romans*,Chapter 7.
2. Charles Spurgeon, *The Soul Winner* (Wm. B. Eerdmans Publishing, 1989), p. 278.

about doctrinal and ethical matters, such as baptism or church leadership or the best ways to care for the poor. Consider what gossip you hear from a church member about someone else in the congregation who reveres *this* rather than *that* celebrity preacher. Consider how rare it is to see a believer surrender their rights so as to avoid causing another to stumble (1 Cor. 8–9). Is there any question that God's people often act in worldly ways rather than according to the priorities of God's kingdom? Such divisiveness is a contagion that stunts the church's spiritual development and usefulness. We are right to grieve it.

But there is something more concerning still than the worldliness you and I can observe "out there." Far more troubling is the problem of worldliness "in here," in our own character and conduct. In fact, *your* wordliness is far less dangerous to me than *my* wordliness. Amid all the pleasures of grace that Christ has lavished on me—surrounded by all the evidence of his constant care and provision—so often I give in to worldliness in my thoughts, attitudes, and actions. That's what troubles me most.

So, what's the answer? What am I to do? What are you to do?

We must return to Paul's key principle. His driving concern in Colossians 3:1–4 is that individual believers *and* whole congregations fix their mind on heaven. He calls believers to go beyond mere Christ-centered words and to practice Christ-centered living. He wants us to experience the full privileges of belonging to an all-sufficient Savior—body and mind and heart and soul. And he wants us to do that together.

As Paul calls believers to be heavenly minded, he's honest about the challenges they will face in doing so. Don't believe me? Well, just keep reading in Colossians 3:5–4:1 and observe all the obstacles and tensions he names! Because of how grueling it can be to cultivate heavenly mindedness, it's vital that we see why it is worth the struggle. In the following chapters, we'll look at three major motivations and incentives Paul gives to spur us on.

PART 2

The Case for Being Heavenly Minded

3

We Are Fit for Heaven

In 1982, the *Miami Herald* printed a story about sixty-six-year-old Yvonne Mary Henderson.[1] For seventeen years, Yvonne Mary Henderson lived in the streets of Miami, Florida. The newspaper article referred to her as a "bag lady." She slept in the streets, fought off muggers and abusers, and scrounged around for food. For seventeen years. But in 1982, some social workers began interacting with her, and soon discovered something truly remarkable: Yvonne Mary Henderson was the heiress of a massive fortune and had money in

---

1. Source: https://www.upi.com/Archives/1982/06/10/Old-bag-lady-is-rich-daughter-of-dead-British-diplomat/7861392529600/ (June 10, 1982).

banks all over the world. Her father had served as a high-ranking diplomat in the British Foreign Office and held great social prominence. Perhaps the most surprising part of the story is that her true identity wasn't news to her. She'd been telling people for years that she actually was an important heiress, but no one believed her. Nor did she do anything to take advantage of the wealth that was legally hers. She just kept on living in the streets.

One of the greatest daily challenges we face is to believe what God has told us about our new identity in Christ and to live according to it. The first incentive Paul gives believers to set our minds on heaven is that we are fit for there: "you have been raised with Christ" (Col. 3:1). Heaven is where those who have been united to Christ belong. Our new identity in Christ has suited us for citizenship in heaven.

A common reason we Christians don't mature in our spiritual lives is that we don't embrace our new identity, either personally or as a body of believers. We may affirm with our lips that we have been made co-heirs with Christ to a colossal inheritance, but we choose to "live in the streets" like "bag ladies." We revert to our old, pre-Christ identity and don't take advantage of all he's purchased for us by his blood. When we're filled with dread, we sometimes indulge that fear rather than resist it. When we're burdened with shame and guilt, we sometimes fail to trust our Father's forgiveness that he's granted us in Christ. When we're marginalized by others for following Christ, we forget that our Savior was marginalized too and promises to bless those who follow in his steps (Matt. 5:10–12).

United to Christ

Paul's opening "if" in Colossians 3:1 draws on what he has already established about believers' new identity. Who are we? Believers in Jesus Christ are "saints" (holy ones) who have been incorporated "in Christ" into God's family. We are the Father's adopted children (Col. 1:2–3). The moment we first believed the gospel, God the Father "delivered us from the domain of darkness and transferred us to the kingdom of his beloved Son, in whom we have redemption, the forgiveness of sins" (Col. 1:13–14). This is stunning! God transformed our very nature, making us "saints" in Christ and citizens of his kingdom. On what basis? Through the Lord Jesus' blood that he shed on the cross (Col. 1:20–21).

The Lord's reconciling work enables believers to experience intimate, direct fellowship with him and, through him, with one another: "Christ in you, the hope of glory" (Col. 1:27).

These aspects of Christian salvation come together in our *union with Christ*. Believers have been filled in Christ, in whom all the fullness of God was pleased to dwell (Col. 2:9–10; see 1:19–20). Through faith, we're joined to Christ in his death, burial, and resurrection (Col. 2:12, 20; 3:1, 3–4; Rom. 6:2–11). Well then, Paul argues, if we truly are united to Christ, we ought to live like it, right? It is only natural that believers should set our minds on things above because we've been made fit for heaven—not simply as individuals, but as a body of believers. It's who we truly are and where we truly belong.

A New Identity, Fixed in Christ

Our generation is no stranger to discussions about identity. The only way you can avoid talking about identity is by sticking your head in the sand. Really deep in the sand. But even though we're living in a world obsessed with "identity," our world can't offer any real solutions to the identity crises that so many are painfully experiencing.

Yes, lots of elements of human self-understanding are fluid, seasonal, and dependent on circumstances. But the Bible teaches us that the most fundamental aspects of Christian identity are firmly fixed. It's folly to look anywhere other than Christ to discover who we really are. Contrary to the world's clamoring voices, human beings don't have to "find themselves" or manufacture their own significance. We aren't the sum of our self-expression or of our experiences, positive or negative. Each human being is the personal handiwork of the Lord Jesus Christ, created for him, for his glory (Col. 1:15–17). Our ordinary lives are infused with extraordinary significance. The one who made us is the only one who can make us whole. Our Creator and Redeemer alone possesses the authority to define us and the power to reconcile us, to Christ and in Christ.

To become spiritually mature, we must embrace our new identity. Everything else in Colossians 3 logically flows from Paul's starting point in verse 1 about our identity in Christ. The character of our Christian life, including our heavenly mindedness, flows directly from our unity with Christ, both personally and corporately. That means that the wellspring of becoming more Christ-like is a growing, dynamic relationship with Jesus Christ. We find our life's purpose and highest privilege in knowing and treasuring the eternal Christ, to whom we belong by grace.

In an age of identity politics, believers have an immense opportunity to demonstrate the gospel's transformative power. That happens as we embrace and enjoy our new identity in Christ. If you're a believer, what might it look like today for you to take hold of this privilege that you are fit for heaven? How might you make progress in listening to what God tells you in the Scriptures about who you are and letting him dictate your self-understanding? And how might you lovingly communicate to your neighbors how your fixed identity in Christ stabilizes you and causes you to flourish?

Believer, this world is not your ultimate home. You're just passing through. So, you won't ever find satisfaction by setting your mind here, on what's below. The very God who made you has made you whole in Christ. He has made you fit for heaven.

4

Our Savior Is in Heaven

When I attend one of my nieces' or nephews' sporting events, there are usually lots of other kids on the field too. But there's only one kid I'm really watching, and I don't take my eyes off that kid. Why? It's simple: I love those rascal relatives of mine! Who I love determines where I fix my eyes. My heart controls my sight.

Not only are you and I fit for heaven, but our Savior is there right now "seated at the right hand of God" (Col. 3:1; Eph. 1:20–23; 2:6). And we don't want to take our eyes off him! What amazing motivation for being heavenly minded. We are to seek the things that are above because the Lord Jesus is reigning over all things *from heaven*. Our glorious, incarnate Savior is there, and he is our life. So our heart must control our sight. We must strive to make progress in heavenly mindedness not only because of who *we* are in him, but because of who *he* is and because of where he is.

Losing sight of Jesus

But there's a problem. A big one. We Christians sometimes lose our confidence in Christ. Most often, it's subtly and gradually that we begin doubting his ability to satisfy us. We don't give up on Jesus all together; rather, we start imagining that, in addition to Christ, we need some other thing to complete us and give us purpose. We imagine that we need a happy marriage and family, a good therapist, a lively social life, a meaningful job, financial success, a good professional reputation, or an effective ministry. Oh, we give credit to Jesus for these good things but deep down we believe Jesus alone cannot satisfy us or make us whole. We start putting some of our confidence in other things, other people, or in our own spiritual and moral performance. Sometimes these other things begin to thrill us more than Christ. They promise to fill us up. They make our lives feel meaningful and significant, or else their absence leaves us feeling empty and insignificant.

Remember that Paul is writing to a local church that is currently plagued by false teachers advocating "Jesus plus" religion. This group is claiming that maturing in the faith, and securing God's full approval, requires more than just receiving and walking in Christ. They are teaching that those in Christ must also strive for some impressive, super-spiritual knowledge and adhere to certain religious practices. The Colossian believers practiced some of these rituals before becoming Christians. And, tragically, some of them have begun to combine their new Christian faith with old religious ideas and habits from their culture. They have a "Jesus plus" faith. Why? Because they have become persuaded that Jesus isn't enough for a person's complete salvation and fullness of life.

The "Jesus plus" mindset that continues to grip individuals and churches today has only one explanation: *we've lost sight of who Jesus really is*. Whenever we doubt Jesus' sufficiency, it's a sure sign that we're not grasping his supremacy. We're not seeing God's beloved Son as he really is. We're failing to recognize his holiness, his sheer awesomeness, his fierce love for his people, and his glorious Lordship over all things. That's why, near the beginning of his letter, Paul sets the Colossians' gaze on Christ (Col. 1:15–23). The Colossians desperately need this renewed vision of who the Lord Jesus is and what he achieved on the cross. Paul lifts their eyes once more to the supreme and beloved Son.

We too need God to open the eyes of our heart to show us Christ in his resplendent glory, "seated at the right hand of God." There, in heaven, the Lord is reigning over all things and interceding for the saints (Rom. 8:34). Only by seeing King Jesus for who he truly is will we be convinced that he's enough for us. It's as we recognize his supremacy over *all* life that we'll trust his sufficiency in *our* life. No one who sees the ascended Son with the eyes of faith can, in their right mind, imagine that they need to add *anything* to his saving work.

Seeking Jesus

I mentioned that I like to show up for my nieces' and nephews' sporting matches. When I'm there, my role is simply to watch. (And occasionally to shout.) But in the Christian life, we're called to much more than passive observation. Christian formation isn't a "spectator sport." We're to get in the game!

That's why Paul urges the Colossians to do more than *see* this glorious Christ in heaven. He calls them to *seek* him. Specifically, Paul charges them to "seek the things that are above, where Christ is, seated at the right hand of God" (3:1). The fact that we *can* seek Christ confirms the powerful working of God in our salvation. In Christ, believers are set free from slavish service of lesser, earthly ambitions—ambitions that leave us emptier the longer we chase them. Christ liberates us to delight in him and labor for the gospel's advance. Since Christ reigns supreme, it's only fitting that seeking him and pleasing him will trump all other aims and relativize all other pursuits, putting them in their rightful place below this ultimate and enduring pursuit.

But how can we know if we are truly seeking what is above, where Christ is? You can't just examine what you say. You've got to go much deeper than that. You've got to look at what fills your days and preoccupies your thoughts. Look at what you want out of life. Look at what most captures your imagination. Look at how regularly you are setting Christ before your eyes by meditating on the Scriptures. Look at what you would be most devastated to lose—is it Christ?

In Colossians 3, Paul is getting at something more fundamental than our behavior. He is after our heart. He is talking about our deepest motivations and loyalties. He is saying that every person who is raised with Christ must focus the desires of his or her heart on heavenly realities. Paul calls us to orient our passions, our will, our aspirations, our dreams according to the priorities of heaven where our ascended Savior reigns in exalted glory. As John Wesley wrote, "Whosoever will reign with Christ in heaven, must have Christ reigning in him on earth."[1]

That means we believers don't live to manage our image. We don't live to make everyone around us happy. We don't live for success and prosperity in our workplace. We don't invest most of our mental and physical energy into carefully curating our bodies or our homes. Neither do we live for our families; their earthly wellbeing, pleasure, and success do not occupy the central place in our hearts. We don't even live to become a dynamic

---

1. John Wesley, *The Works of the Rev. John Wesley*, A.M., ed. John Emory, volume VI (New York: J. Emory and B. Waugh, 1831), p. 137.

Bible teacher, the most effective evangelist in our local church, or the author of a bestselling Christian book. In fact, we don't live for ourselves at all.

Or do we?

A divided heart

If you're anything like me, your heart is often divided, and sometimes deceptively so. At times we Christians aren't even aware when our driving ambitions are self- rather than Christ-centered. Our commitment to religious activities can blind us to our own worldliness. We religious folk can fool ourselves into imagining that we are consistently, fundamentally motivated by Christ's glory and his gospel's advance. But, in reality, sometimes what *actually* inspires our religious activity is something quite different, something hypocritical. We want to make a name for ourselves, to be noticed and valued by people and leaders we deem important, to earn our right standing with God, to make up for our past failures, or to feel needed. A person may undergo extensive training in evangelism, steward his or her wealth for the good of the poor, craft an impressive theological library, preach gripping sermons, and even contribute to others' spiritual development. But it's quite possible to do all that with a cold heart (1 Cor. 13:1–3). How so? Because we can perform any of these religious activities in a spirit that marginalizes Jesus Christ in our heart. Worldliness can lurk in our religious conduct, even without our fully realizing it.

The solution to such a divided heart is not to look inward to ourselves or outward to people around us, but upward to heaven, where Christ is. God beckons his children to let him expose our divided heart and then empower us for wholehearted devotion (see Ps. 19:12–14). Of course, until he returns, we won't look to Christ with perfect consistency. Nor will we ever reach a point of independence in which we no longer need God's help to keep our focus on heaven. But God provides all we need to plod along in repentance, making progress in setting our minds on what is above. He gives us himself, the Scriptures, local-church fellowship, the Lord's Supper, prayer, and deeds of mercy (see Acts 2:42–47). God uses these gifts to train our hearts to seek Christ, who reigns from heaven and can alone be trusted to fill us.

5

We Are Going to Heaven

In Colossians 3, Paul gives a final motivation for cultivating heavenly mindedness. Not only are we fit for heaven, not only is our Savior there, but we are going there too: "For you have died, and your life is hidden with Christ in God. When Christ who is your life appears, then you also will appear with him in glory" (Col. 3:3–4). Heaven is the believer's ultimate destination. Our salvation's sure outcome ought to fill us with unflinching assurance and joy. This final incentive is deep and rich—encompassing two glorious truths—Jesus is coming to us in glory and we are going to him in glory.

Jesus Is Coming to Us in Glory

One of my good friends ministered among university students for several years. Once a year, the students and staff workers would go away for a weekend retreat. At those retreats, they would study the Bible together and gather for various breakout sessions on timely topics. On their arrival, each student would receive a brochure that listed the titles for these sessions. On one occasion, a new Christian named Elizabeth came along. Soon after arriving for the retreat, Elizabeth bounded suddenly into the room where most of the students were chatting casually. She was shouting, "Jesus is coming back? Jesus is coming back? *Jesus is coming back!*"

It took my friend a few moments to work out what had happened. One of the retreat breakout sessions was titled "Jesus Is Coming Back Soon." Apparently, the person who had shared the gospel with Elizabeth failed to inform her of this critical part of the message—namely, that Jesus will be returning to collect his people and bring them home to heaven! On reading the simple news of Jesus' personal, imminent return, Elizabeth absolutely lost it with joy.

Elizabeth's wild, raucous exuberance is exactly right. It is exactly *sane*. But sometimes we believers go about our business in the opposite way, as if uncertain about how our story ends. Ours is a happy ending. Have we forgotten that our King is coming back to make all things new, and that he wants to find his people ready for him, going about his business?

Believers should cultivate heavenly mindedness because we are deeply, forever longing for the Lord Jesus' personal, glorious return. We are those who have "turned to God from idols to serve the living and true God, and to wait for his Son from heaven" (1 Thes. 1:9–10). The very Christ we proclaim today is the Christ we soon shall see face to face at his coming.

We ought to live every moment with the expectation that Christ will return. To what extent do you live this way? Do you contemplate Christ's return? Is your mindset one of eager expectation to see Christ face to face?

One barrier that keeps us from ever-deepening joy over beholding Christ at his return relates to how we conceptualize heaven. Sometimes when we believers speak of heaven, we mostly emphasize heaven's secondary benefits, such as freedom from pain and heartache. Tragically, our longing for heaven can become more about what heaven lacks (that is, suffering) than who it has (that is, God). When we lose sight of who Christ is, heaven becomes to us more about the pain that is absent than the Savior who is present. We distort "heavenly mindedness" into mere escapism. But a Christ-less heaven is no heaven at all. Heaven's central feature is God himself. Scripture calls us to anticipate fellowship with our beloved Savior as the all-surpassing joy, better even than being reunited with beloved saints who have died, though joyful that will be!

If Christ isn't the center of your ambitions for your future in heaven, he won't be the center of your ambitions for your life on earth. If we aren't focused on Christ's return, we'll be enticed by the world's alluring promise of instant gratification. But if we regard Christ as all-sufficient for our earthly and heavenly future, we are empowered to resist the temptation to seek our satisfaction from things below, including from our spiritual and ministry endeavors. Our King's return will satisfy our heart and energize us so that we make "the best use of the time" (Col. 4:5), for his glory.

We Are Going to Jesus in Glory

Don't you love how the good news in our Colossians passage just keeps getting better? Paul goes on to show that our heavenly mindedness isn't only motivated by the hope that, at Jesus' return, he will appear to us in glory, but also that we will appear with him in glory. He will bring us home to heaven, glorified. God bids his children to aspire for heavenly things because he wants to bless us from heaven and, ultimately, *with* heaven.

Paul's language in Colossians 3:3 is very interesting. The word Paul uses for "hidden" is a Greek word from which we get "cryptic." Paul is saying that we are now cryptically in Christ. To the world, we are incognito. Our identity is concealed from them. The world thinks we're just ordinary human beings. They have no idea that we believers are actually sons and daughters of the Most High God. But, oh boy, are they going to find out! When Christ returns, not only will his identity be made fully known but so will ours (Col. 3:4). On that great day, all people will see that Jesus Christ is the Messiah, and we are his siblings. What a day that will be!

A few years ago, I attended a friend's wedding in Illinois. She is a believer who married a dear

Christian brother. The bride grew up in an extremely difficult home, full of drug abuse, neglect, hatred, and contentious lawsuits. As a result of her home life's dramatic instability, she had struggled her whole life to understand who she is and how she fits in the world. Yet when she walked down the aisle to her soon-to-be husband, she was one of the most joyful brides I have ever seen. Her joy affected the whole congregation, including the minister officiating at the service. When the bride finally arrived to her groom, tears were streaming down the minister's face. After the ceremony, I asked the minister what had moved him so deeply. He said, tearfully, "Finally, she belongs. Her whole life she's struggled and longed for security. She'll still have much to work out; marriage won't solve her problems. But for the first time in her life, she belongs to someone who cherishes her and will lay down his life for her."

This captures some of the gospel's drama, does it not? But the surety of our belonging to Christ can be difficult to trust. Unsettling doubts can lurk in our hearts. Sometimes, deep down, we fear God will reject us one day. We fear that even though he accepted us in Christ in the past, he might change his mind the more he gets to know us. We imagine that we're in a probationary position, like some kind of servant who can be fired at will if our productivity isn't up to snuff. We *say* that we're God's adopted children, but we *live* as if our full adoption were pending a future performance review.

But what's the truth? If you have been united to Christ by faith, no sin or failure of yours catches your Father off guard. He isn't surprised by your weakness, your inadequacy, your insecurity, your fear. He has accounted for it all. He understood your full condition when he made you co-heir with his Son. If you're a believer in Christ, your life is hidden with Christ in God. Your safety in Christ is as secure, as indissoluble, as Christ's own union with God the Father. And when Christ appears, you also will appear with him in glory. Blessed assurance!

Remember the Lord Jesus' encouragement to his disciples:

> *Let not your hearts be troubled. Believe in God; believe also in me. In my Father's house are many rooms. If it were not so, would I have told you that I go to prepare a place for you? And if I go and prepare a place for you, I will come again and will*

take you to myself, that where I am you may be also (John 14:1–3).

The church's story culminates in a wedding that will be far more dramatic than the one I just described. Christ, the bridegroom, will present the church, his bride, to the Father with great joy (Jude 24). Christ will bring his bride into their everlasting home together. Cultivating Christ-centered heavenly mindedness leads to an outcome far exceeding anything we could ask for or imagine. When Christ appears, every one of us who has been raised with him by faith will be glorified, fully matured into his image because we will see him as he is (1 John 3:2). Our incarnate Lord will give us imperishable bodies suited for everlasting life with him in the new heavens and new earth (1 Cor. 15:35–57). Come quickly, Lord Jesus!

Meanwhile, we wait in hope.

We also wait alert to danger. Just as there were false teachers among the church at Colossae, so there are false teachers in our generation. They will try to convince you of a "Jesus plus" spirituality. They'll advocate self-made solutions for spiritual growth, solutions that appear wise but lack real spiritual power (Col. 2:23). They'll try to persuade you to divide up the pie chart of spiritual fullness: to try and add your moral performance, religious activities, self-help fads, civic activism, or ministry effectiveness to Jesus' saving work. They'll try to entrap you in judgmentalism, spiritual elitism, and exclusion of others.

Run! Don't have anything to do with them. Christ, who is seated at the Father's right hand, guarantees your glorious, everlasting future in heaven. There's nothing to add to his mighty work. Just rejoice in it! Fix your eyes on him. Set your mind on what he *has* done for you, what he *is* doing for you, and where he *will* take you to spend eternity with him:

> *If then you have been raised with Christ, seek the things that are above, where Christ is, seated at the right hand of God. Set your minds on things that are above, not on things that are on earth. For you have died, and your life is hidden with Christ in God. When Christ who is your life appears, then you also will appear with him in glory (Col. 3:1–4).*

Questions for Discussion and Reflection

1. How confident are you that you have been "raised with Christ" (Col 3:1)? Why?

2. Paul urges the Colossians to cultivate heavenly mindedness because of their new identity in Christ: they are fit for heaven. When is it most difficult for you to live out your new identity in Christ? What have you found of practical help to resist the temptation to go back to the identity you had before becoming a Christian?

3. Paul also urges the Colossians to cultivate heavenly mindedness because their Savior is there in heaven. In what area of life are you most tempted to seek something other than Christ for your ultimate satisfaction? Christ is seated at the right hand of the Father in heaven. How does this truth encourage you to seek him alone in this specific area of your life?

4. Finally, Paul urges the Colossians to cultivate heavenly mindedness because they are going to heaven: Jesus is returning to them in glory, and they are returning to Jesus in glory. Identify a season in your life when God especially strengthened your assurance of your heavenly future with him. What, in particular, did God use to assure you? In what areas do you need fresh assurance today about the ultimate outcome of your salvation?

5. Read Revelation 21–22. What are the striking differences between what this passage emphasizes about heaven and what people in our culture often emphasize about "the afterlife"? In what specific ways does this biblical vision of the new heaven and new earth encourage you today to embrace and enjoy Christ's full sufficiency?

10Publishing is the publishing house of **10ofThose**.
It is committed to producing quality Christian resources that are biblical and accessible.

www.10ofthose.com is our online retail arm selling thousands of quality books at discounted prices.

For information contact: **info@10ofthose.com**
or check out our website: **www.10ofthose.com**